# The Perilous Tale of Gus

(Anna Barbosa)

Written by: Gus & his Mom
Illustrated by: K.W. Schon

Archway Publishing books may be ordered through booksellers or by contacting:

Archway Publishing
1663 Liberty Drive
Bloomington, IN 47403
www.archwaypublishing.com
844-669-3957

ISBN: 978-1-4808-9811-0 (sc)
ISBN: 978-1-4808-9810-3 (hc)
ISBN: 978-1-4808-9809-7 (e)

Print information available on the last page.

Archway Publishing rev. date: 01/28/2021

Hello there! I'm Gus. I am a happy dog.

I have a mom who loves me and gives me fun toys. I have my very own food bowl with my very own name on it. I have a special bed for napping on the porch, and I smile in my sleep while I listen to kids playing and birds singing and squirrels chattering.

Yes, I am a lucky dog! But, I wasn't always this lucky.

When I was little, I had no one to love me or take care of me. It took a long time, and some special people, to make me the happy and healthy dog I am today.

Let me tell you about it!

When I was a tiny puppy, I had no home, but I lived underneath an old, old truck. It was rusty and red and rickety, but it kept me dry in the big booming thunderstorms.

I didn't have a dog bowl then, so I had to scrounge for food. I checked the trash cans every night and the dumpsters every day. I was always hungry, and I felt so alone.

On the day I made my first friend ever, I was trying to tug a trash bag out of the dumpster to find a snack. Tug, tug, tug - and then riiiip! The bag burst and I bounced backwards.

I heard a giggle, and someone took the banana peel off my nose. It was a little girl, and my first friend. She patted my head and called me cute. I didn't know I was cute!

She even gave me my very own collar, a beautiful blue shoelace from her own sneaker. I loved it then, but I didn't love it later—you'll see why.

We were friends for awhile, but the little girl and her family left one day, in a little car stuffed full with their things. She waved to me, and I wagged my tail to say goodbye, but I felt sad inside. What did I do wrong?

Have you ever felt sad inside, but tried to act happy?

But don't worry, I made my second friend soon after that. It was the day of a big thunderstorm. The rickety red truck was shaking with every boom of thunder and I squeezed my eyes shut with every bright flash of lightning. Suddenly...

. . . OoPH!

...BAM! A wet furry cannonball crashed right into me!

I jumped to my feet
with a yelp,

and the little cannonball
unrolled itself

and shook its wet fur.

It was a tiny white and gray terrier!

As the thunder boomed and lightning crashed, we touched noses and introduced ourselves. This was Trixie, my second friend.

Now I lived under the truck with Trixie. I wasn't so lonely, but boy was I hungry!

Have you ever been hungry? So hungry your stomach growls and aches?

Trixie and I spent our days searching, searching, searching for food. We had to be smart. There were fast cars, and busy bikes, and big-footed people who didn't like "strays."

When I was little and cute, people were nicer when they saw me. Now I was growing up, and I wasn't very cute anymore. Those big-footed people didn't want me around so they shooed me away.

Remember the shoelace I told you about? My pretend collar? Well, I got bigger, and the shoelace got tighter. I couldn't get it off! It hurt, hurt, hurt all the time. I couldn't help it that my whole head got bigger and bigger because the shoe-lace grew tighter and tighter around my neck.

Trixie still cared about me. She was a true friend.

Trixie and I thought we'd live together under the old truck, forever!

But one day, everything changed. It was the day I made my third friend, but it didn't start out well.

Trixie and I were going to the restaurant dumpster across the street. Sometimes they had old croissants and expired milk cartons and even half-eaten peanut butter sandwiches. Have you ever had a peanut butter sandwich? They're delicious!

Trixie started across the road, but she didn't see the fast yellow car coming. It came so fast, I didn't have time to yelp, so I did the only thing I could think of: I ran into the road and pushed her out of the way.

Trixie was ok, but the car knocked me flying.

OUCH!

Oh, my leg hurt! And I was so scared.

The car tires screeching made people turn and look. Now they were running towards me! I looked around for Trixie, but someone was already holding her tight. She yelped and squirmed to try to get to me.

Those people were running to help me, but I didn't know that! I thought maybe I was in trouble, so I ran away as fast as I could.

Have you ever tried to hide when you thought you were in trouble?

I thought if I could hide for long enough, the people would go away. But those people wanted to help me so badly, they just kept looking!

I was under my truck, hurting and tired, when suddenly a delicious smell filled my nose. A treat dropped to the ground. A treat! I hadn't seen one in ages. It smelled delicious!

As I crawled toward the treat, a smiling face peeked down under the truck.

TREAT

"It's ok!" he said softly, not coming close, but holding out his hand for me to smell. "We're here to help you."

And that's when I made my third friend! And then my fourth, and my fifth...and well, I can't count as high as the number of friends I made that day. But it was a lot! Can you believe that so many people cared about a dog that nobody wanted?

And now? Now I am a happy dog!

The veterinarian, and a lot of other kind people, took care of my hurt neck from the shoelace, and my hurt leg from the car...and my hungry stomach, too!

Best of all, they found me the greatest mom in the world—she promised to take care of me and play with me and love me forever!

Who do you love most in the world?

Someone to love is a very special thing. I think every dog should have someone to love. That's what makes me a happy dog!

That, and tasty treats. Yum!

A Note from Anna and Katie:

Gus and Trixie are real dogs, and this is a true story! Gus can't tell us exactly what life was like as a puppy on the streets, or exactly what happened to him when he lived there, so some of our story is a best guess at what happened. We do know that Gus was found very hurt and sick, and needed lots of care and love by lots of people to get better. Many people have been interested in Gus's story - he's a little bit famous! Gus was voted the 2019 Hero Shelter Dog by the American Humane society, and has helped tell lots of people about life as a homeless dog. For more about Gus and Houston K911 Rescue, and to find out how you can help homeless dogs, visit Houstonk911rescue.org—and be sure to tell your friends all about Gus!

Printed in the United States
By Bookmasters